D0776763

Your
Faith
Walk

Wisdom and Affirmations
on the Path to Personal Power

FROM THE EDITORS OF

ESSENCE

FOREWORD BY
Vanessa K. De Luca

CONTENTS

ESSENCE

EDITOR-IN-CHIEF Vanessa K. De Luca
DEPUTY MANAGING EDITOR Dawnie Walton
CREATIVE DIRECTOR Erika N. Perry
EDITORIAL PROJECTS DIRECTOR Patrik Henry Bass
EDITORIAL OPERATIONS DIRECTOR Denolyn Carroll

ESSENCE Presents **YOUR FAITH WALK: WISDOM AND AFFIRMATIONS ON THE PATH TO PERSONAL POWER**

EDITOR Patrik Henry Bass
EDITORIAL CONSULTANT Cheryl D. Woodruff
DESIGN DIRECTOR Pinda D. Romain
PHOTO DIRECTOR Adreinne Waheed
PRODUCTION MANAGER Raphael Joa
REPORTERS/WRITERS Bridgette Bartlett Royall, Nazenet Habtezghi
COPY EDITOR Christopher Carbone

CONTENT CREDITS
Lucille Clifton, "female" and "why some people be mad at me sometimes" from The Collected Poems of Lucille Clifton. Copyright © 1987 by Lucille Clifton. Reprinted with the permission of The Permissions Company, Inc., on behalf of BOA Editions Ltd., boaeditions.org. "A Letter to Fred" copyright © 1989 by Lucille Clifton. Reprinted by permission of Curtis Brown, Ltd. "Heritage" copyright © 1992 by Lisa Bond Brewer. Reprinted by permission of the author. Community volunteer and protester images used for journalistic purposes.

All of the quotes in this book, except for the foreword, are excerpts from content that previously appeared in ESSENCE Magazine.

SPECIAL THANKS
Michelle Ebanks, Marie D. Brown, Carina A. Rosario, Amy Glickman, Andrea M. Jackson, Monique Manso, Armando Correa, Sidney Clifton, Dawn Abbott, Pamela Edwards Christiani, Akkida McDowell, Grace White, Michael Rowe, Joiee Thorpe

THIS BOOK IS LOVINGLY DEDICATED TO JONELL NASH

TIME INC. BOOKS
PUBLISHER Margot Schupf
VICE PRESIDENT, FINANCE Vandana Patel
EXECUTIVE DIRECTOR, MARKETING SERVICES Carol Pittard
EXECUTIVE DIRECTOR, BUSINESS DEVELOPMENT Suzanne Albert
EXECUTIVE DIRECTOR, MARKETING Susan Hettleman
EXECUTIVE PUBLISHING DIRECTOR Megan Pearlman

ASSOCIATE DIRECTOR OF PUBLICITY Courtney Greenhalgh
ASSISTANT GENERAL COUNSEL Simone Procas
ASSISTANT DIRECTOR, SPECIAL SALES Ilene Schreider
ASSISTANT DIRECTOR, FINANCE Christine Font
ASSISTANT PUBLISHING DIRECTOR Susan Chodakiewicz
SENIOR MANAGER, SALES MARKETING Danielle Costa
ASSOCIATE PRODUCTION MANAGER Kimberly Marshall
ASSOCIATE PREPRESS MANAGER Alex Voznesenskiy
ASSOCIATE PROJECT MANAGER Amy Mangus

EDITORIAL DIRECTOR Stephen Koepp
ART DIRECTOR Gary Stewart
SENIOR EDITORS Roe D'Angelo, Alyssa Smith
MANAGING EDITOR Matt DeMazza
COPY CHIEF Rina Bander
DESIGN MANAGER Anne-Michelle Gallero
ASSISTANT MANAGING EDITOR Gina Scauzillo
EDITORIAL ASSISTANT Courtney Mifsud

ISBN 10: 1-61893-163-6
ISBN 13: 978-1-61893-163-4
Library of Congress Control Number: 2015931372
Copyright © 2015 Essence Communications Inc.

FOREWORD

VANESSA K. DE LUCA

This year marks a special milestone for ESSENCE: our 45th anniversary. Whether you still have that very first May 1970 issue featuring the flawless and fearless cover model Barbara Cheeseborough, or you are a new visitor to the magazine, or ESSENCE.com, we hope that the words and images we present daily and monthly continue to inform and inspire you.

In looking back over four and a half decades of our rich history, the Editors of ESSENCE have chronicled the extraordinary progress Black women have made since the magazine was born. Indeed, ESSENCE women have served in extraordinary professional roles and leadership positions in our nation's capital from congresswoman to senator, secretary of state to first lady, and have taken African-Americans' fight against injustice to the media, the streets, the classroom and the courthouse.

ESSENCE women have transformed how global business is done as CEOs and C-Suite office holders and dared to stake their claim as risk-taking entrepreneurs. We have blazed trails in Hollywood picking up Oscars, dozens of Emmys, creating, directing, and starring in groundbreaking dramas and comedies on screens big and small. We have created an unparalleled music culture from vibrant neighborhood church choirs to record shattering international concert tours "womaned" by Grammy-award–winning artists who have rocked the beat of the world.

ESSENCE women have championed a cultural revolution that created respect and honor for the diverse expressions of Black women's beauty, glamour and style. And we never, ever did it alone. We did it with words of encouragement from our sisters in our kitchens, at church, in hair and nail salons, during our coffee breaks, Sunday brunch or family reunions. Because no matter where ESSENCE women gather, we always hold each other's hands and heal each other's hearts.

Your Faith Walk: Wisdom and Affirmations on the Path to Personal Power mirrors these experiences and reflects ESSENCE's uncompromising commitment to Black women's empowerment. To produce this volume of our collective wisdom that bears witness to our journey— our editors went back into our archives and discovered a profound chorus of voices including Susan L. Taylor, Audre Lorde, Mellody Hobson, Iyanla Vanzant, Oprah and courageous readers just like you.

Over the years, like you, I have pinned many of these life-changing quotes on my college dorm wall, on my desk at work or my refrigerator at home and continually shared them with my sisters. Taken together, every word in this book provides evidence of how and why we've come so far—together—and provides sustenance for the march forward into our individual and collective greatness.

Your Faith Walk is designed to be that unforgettable whisper in your ear that motivates you to keep going no matter what internal or external challenge you may face. Remember, without you, there is no us. It is our duty, responsibility and joy to remind you that your path is filled with unlimited possibilities and that ESSENCE will always walk with you every step of the way.

PREFACE

SUSAN L. TAYLOR

FAITH

"*Strange thing about faith.* We only know the degree to which we really believe in God's love when our faith is tested. And it seems that abundant faith often flows from doubt and fear. It is so with me. During times of crisis I've often doubted myself and felt very much alone; I've seen just how shaky my faith can be. But it's also been in my darkest hours—when my reasoning mind fails to see the larger cycles at work, when my faith is like a dying ember—that I've grown in the awareness of God's tremendous power. The seeds of faith are always within us, but sometimes it takes a crisis to nourish them and encourage their growth.

Just like you, I want to avoid personal pain and suffering as much as possible. But I also know that each of our dilemmas provides us with an opportunity to discover deeper levels of truth and build greater strengths. When it's history we can look back on a crisis and understand why we needed the experience. But we must learn to trust that Divine Order is working on our behalf and that good is on the other side of the obstacle while we're confronting it. That's living our faith!"

"FAITH IS INNER FREEDOM,

the only freedom. Nothing can free us in the world until we feel it from within. You need faith to stake your place in this world. You need a security that neither people nor earthly things offer in order to stand your ground.

FAITH IS OUR GREATEST TOOL

IN LIFE:

IT NEVER EVER FAILS."

11

THERE'S NOTHING BETTER THAN LOVE

How's your love life these days? And by love, I'm not just speaking to those who are coupled up. Besides, who says that you can only have love in your life with a partner? Despite the messages in romantic comedies and heartwarming commercials on the big and small screen, I believe love has no limits. Love is powerful enough to reach beyond two people.

I'm still moved by a recent celebration for a very special friend. Like all of us at some point, at the moment she is weathering an extremely challenging season in her life. Nearly 30 of her friends, of all ages and life stages, came together for dinner and cocktails to let her know how much value and joy she brings to so many lives. Yes, there were tears. However, as we parted there was also confirmation that the love we share with others is as powerful as the love we share with one.

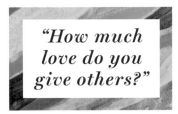

"How much love do you give others?"

How much love do you give to others, and how much are you allowing others to show you? How often do you look your children, parents or significant other in the eyes and say, "I love you"? How many times in a month do you hug it out with friends or colleagues you cherish? And in what ways are you sharing your love by donating an hour of your time and talents to help others in even the smallest way?

As we were putting the finishing touches on this issue, we learned of Nelson Mandela's passing. The outpouring of love for Madiba expressed globally, across generations and cultures, proves that if we have the courage, strength and sheer tenacity to live our lives with a loving spirit, we can change the world.

Vanessa K. De Luca
Editor-in-Chief
February 14, 2014

female

there is an amazon in us.
she is the secret we do not
have to learn.
the strength that opens us
beyond ourselves.
birth is our birthright.
we smile our mysterious smile.

 LUCILLE CLIFTON

self-love

Mary J. Blige

"LOVE IS A VERB
AND A PROCESS.
THERE ARE VARYING TYPES
AND DEGREES.

ROMANTIC LOVE.
PARENTAL LOVE.
LOVE FOR ONE'S CRAFT.
SELF-LOVE.

MASTERING EACH REQUIRES
TIME AND ENERGY."

REGINA R. ROBERTSON

"Grace has to do with one's deliberate, chosen way of being in this world....For a Black woman, the choice is imperative...

So when she decides I am first a gift—I am the creation of the Creator, and the Creator makes no mistakes, I belong to myself, I live inside this place, it is all of me that lives inside this place, and everything about me belongs to me first—the moment that decision is made, grace enters."

MAYA ANGELOU

"No **magic** formula—no mantra, fad diet, five minute workout or new 'do—is going to make a lasting difference. To create **balance, wholeness,** we must make ourselves our number one priority, giving conscious care to our **body, mind** and **spirit** each day for the rest of our lives. There is no quick fix; **we have to do the work.**"

SUSAN L. TAYLOR

"Caring for myself

is not self-indulgence;

it is self-preservation..."

AUDRE LORDE

"By continually facing these hidden fears and frustrations, you will liberate the wounded little girl inside you. But first you must get in GEAR—grieve, express, analyze and release your loss. Release some of your anxieties by substituting them with reassuring thoughts and words. I claim my passion for living and loving. Love will cast out fear. Then take a moment to breathe slowly, relax and embrace yourself in a loving manner. Assure that unhappy little girl inside you that she is not alone and unloved. Tell her, 'I will love you forever and that's a promise, as an adult, I will keep. You can depend on it.'"

DR. GWENDOLYN GOLDSBY GRANT

25

I am focusing...

I am focusing...

I am focusing...

I am focusing...

...on loving myself. Just as I am. Goodbye feelings of inadequacy and incompleteness, loneliness and pain—all fear inspired—which cannot exist with love."

LOUISE MERIWETHER

"High self-esteem is the greatest gift you can give to yourself...It's self-confidence in the truest sense—not a mask of superiority put on to impress other people, but a deep down feeling of inner worth. It's that voice inside you that says,

I like myself.
I'm good. I'm capable.
I have something
positive to offer myself
and other people."

MONIQUE BURNS

"TO ACHIEVE TOTAL WELL-BEING WE MUST REMIND OURSELVES THAT WE ARE STRONG AND IN CHARGE...

We change our lives by changing our behavior.

YOU'VE GOT TO BELIEVE IN YOUR POWER AND BEGIN TO ACT...

Don't compare yourself with anyone else. Each of us is a divine original, created to do a unique work.

OUR ONLY COMPETITION IS WITH WHO WE WERE YESTERDAY."

SUSAN L. TAYLOR

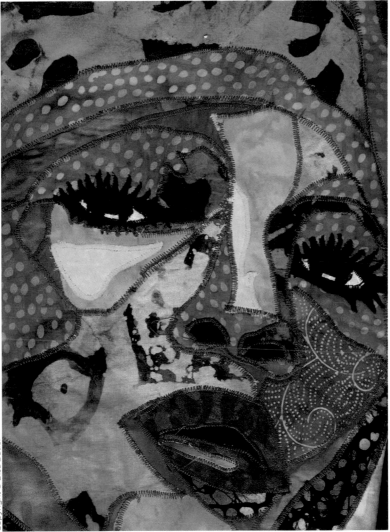

"Never forget
that this is your
ONE,
PRECIOUS LIFE.
YOUR LIFE.

And you have the
POWER
to create your future."

ROBIN ROBERTS

"**Women** who love by their own
inner truths
are willing to discover themselves regardless
of society's condemnation.
Because they possess
self-knowledge,
they lead successful and
creative lives."

DR. GWENDOLYN GOLDSBY GRANT

35

relationships

"Since the very beginning of bedtime stories, little girls have fantasized about a prince. He will ride in and save us from all the painful, evil forces. We watch movies dripping with make-believe romance, and we expect an orange moon, Tiffany's boxes and countless hours of lovemaking. But the reality of romance will keep some of us looking forever. Nobody is perfect. Each and every one of us has issues—with family, with health or money, with past relationships. We all want to be happy and loved, but who are we

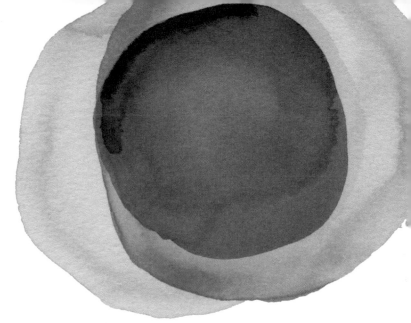

to just sit back and expect it? We have to keep working, keep getting better. That doesn't mean we can't find the perfect partner. It means that the person who is our perfect match won't be perfect at all.

I'm just sayin'."

JILL SCOTT

"It helps if we understand that buried underneath our desire to be rescued by Prince Charming is a basic human longing for an intimate connection with another person who will share in our struggle, who will make us feel everything will be okay, who will affirm that we do indeed deserve to be cared for. Black women do deserve love, nurturing and security, but to foster these in a relationship we must first possess them ourselves."

ZIBA KASHEF

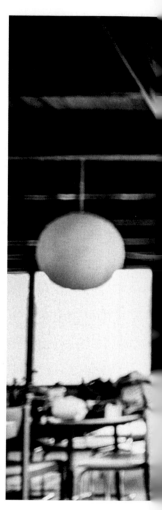

39

"He'll show up on God's schedule—not yours.

In the meantime, continue to enjoy life.

Expose yourself to all sorts of experiences.

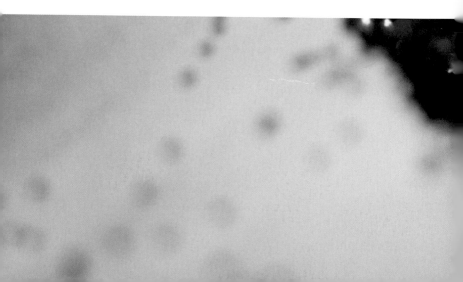

Laugh often and love a lot. Strive to be a person who loves life and wants to share life with someone else. It's the energy of a well-lived life that your soul mate will be attracted to."

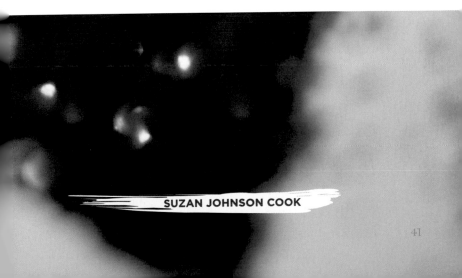

SUZAN JOHNSON COOK

"Love recognizes no barriers.

It jumps hurdles, leaps

fences, penetrates walls

to arrive at its destination

full of hope."

MAYA ANGELOU

black love is...

"They say real love is fading away, but we know better. Not our love. Our love is serious. Our love is as sweet as a cool breeze on a hot, sticky morning. Our love is as wild as a summer rainstorm. Our love touches your lips, caresses your shoulder, rocks you to sleep at night. Our love crackles with life like an old 45 record. Our love grooves hip to hip. Our love leads a nation, with power and promise and hope. Our love endures— it ain't goin' nowhere, no how. Our love is real."

JEANNINE AMBER

"Black
love is a vaccine
against the negativity
that comes with being
Black in America.
It represents
triumph!"

–Donnie S., Chicago

"Black
love is strength,
forgiveness and
tolerance. After ten
years, my guy and
I grow closer
each day."

–Debbie P., Atlanta

Ruby Dee and Ossie Davis

"A trustworthy marriage has weathered temptation and anger and jealousy, resentment and a little bit of selfishness. When you get over and get through that, then maybe you can see the light to love."

RUBY DEE

"Some say we are
responsible for those we love.
Others know we are
responsible for those who love us."

NIKKI GIOVANNI

WE ARE IN

"In order for us to become healthy we have to take charge of the power we have within ourselves.
We can't change anyone else but when we change ourselves we change the way the world relates to us.

CHARGE."

BYLLYE Y. AVERY

A Letter to Fred

Dear Fred,

"It is five years since last I saw you with my eyes. So much has happened. So much to learn, you used to say. So much I took for granted, so much."

...Remember when people warned me against you? The kids and I laugh about that. They can't believe that anyone would suggest I not marry you because of the color of your skin. The world we grew up in is not a world they know. "That boy is too Black," some folks would say... It seems far away, doesn't it? But it's not.

Know what you never told me? I was fat. And old, no, middle-aged. And that men who are my age are after women the age of our daughters—and the size.... I know that I miss the eyes that remembered me at 19. The eyes that saw no difference in me that mattered, the eyes that laughed and said, "Whatever you do, don't lose that behind!"

Lucille and Fred Clifton

...I remember the evening I was fussing in the kitchen about all the time you spent away from us, your family. "We need you," I half-fussed and a half-laughed as I usually did. And you began to cry. I think about that almost every day, your tears as you tried to explain, as you depended on me to see, to understand: "But Lucille, our people need so much!" I'm not sure that I saw then, as much as I might have, but I did know then that I could not have married anyone else; I could not have lived with a man who could not feel and could not cry about our people's need...And I cry, too, and I wish you were here."

LUCILLE CLIFTON

FAT IS A BLACK WOMAN'S ISSUE

"I am one example of the many Black women who are seen as merely fat or greedy, who are called ugly because we fail to fit the image that predominates in magazines and newspapers, on television...while everyone fails to see that we are in pain.

I was constantly perceived as a maternal Black woman by my peers and teachers. I think some people actually visualized themselves clinging to me with their head on my bosom. And why not? The image of the big, strong, nurturing Black woman has existed in print and visual media for years...Unfortunately, this problem solver and eternal-sustainer persona becomes the lifework of many women.

...I no longer accept the role of all-giving nurturer; I'm taking the time to care for

MY OWN NEEDS."

RETHA POWERS

healing

55

"When we truly begin to recognize the power that lies locked in our minds and accept responsibility for all our thoughts, words and actions, our lives will improve and expand in dramatic ways. What a simple principle. But, amazingly, many people have trouble adhering to it, seeking instead to place the blame for their misery on everyone and everything but themselves.

We must remember that physical manifestations are reflections of our joy, happiness, anger, fear, pain and confusion. To attain physical, emotional, mental and spiritual health, we must begin loving ourselves, cleansing our minds and releasing the negative energy that we have stored within us. If we can release negativity, we'll be able to move forward...

*One. Admit your faults.
Two. See yourself as you
want to be.
Three. Pray and affirm.
Four. Make time for
mental house cleaning.
Five. Learn to forgive."*

IYANLA VANZANT

"You can get addicted to pain.
But you can also

GET ADDICTED TO JOY!

…I am sure there is pain waiting in my life.
The whole world situation is painful.
But I am here to tell you that your joy
can equal your pain—it can strip your pain.

…YOU KNOW THE EXPRESSION "UNSPEAKABLE JOY"?

I have unspeakable joy even as I deal with
my anger, sorrow and grief."

ALICE WALKER

59

"With sex, getting older means getting better–knowing what you enjoy, what you don't enjoy, knowing how to give pleasure, knowing how to receive pleasure."

HATTIE GOSSETT

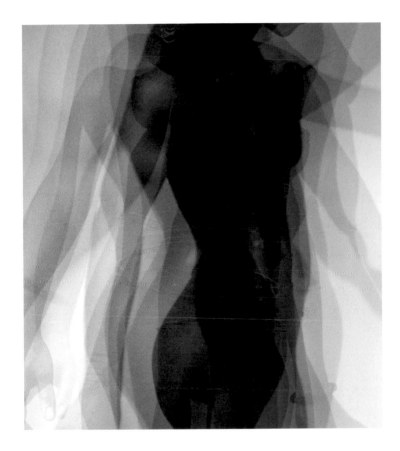

"We don't often have the luxury of slowing down or taking to our beds when we're severely depressed. We're usually forced to keep functioning.

So if someone is
chronically irritable
or angry, she might
be seen as a Sapphire
rather than as having a
serious illness
that is treatable."

DR. BRENDA WADE

"The reward of freeing yourself of old resentments is that you become whole. You begin to understand how faith, mercy and grace are at work in your life."

ZOLEKA ADAMS

Model used for illustration only

Rae Lewis-Thornton

What I have clearly learned is that, unlike people, AIDS does not discriminate. My wish is that all women would realize this and take control of their lives and their bodies. To not use a condom in this day and age is suicide.

"I'm young—32. Well-educated. Professional. Attractive. Smart. I've been drug- and alcohol-free all my life. I'm a Christian. I've never been promiscuous. Never had a one night stand. And I am dying of AIDS. I have been living with the disease for nine years, and people still tell me that I am too pretty and intelligent to have

AIDS. But I do. I discovered I was HIV-positive when I tried to give blood at the office. I have no idea who infected me or how it happened. Still, there is one thing I am absolutely certain of: I'm dying because I had one sexual partner too many. And I'm here to tell you one is all it takes.

But the day I found out my HIV status, I wasn't thinking of dying. I'd already overcome a lot, and I believed there was nothing I couldn't conquer...

Surrendering myself to God is the smartest decision I have made in this odyssey. As I let go of the old person, God created a new one. This new Rae has a purpose. What I discovered was that God uses us in ways not of our own understanding. And once you let go and let God, He reveals the plan. When you accept it, blessings flow."

RAE LEWIS-THORNTON

"We don't call ourselves celibate, we call ourselves smart. AIDS is nothing to play with. We are the first generation to grow up with this 20th century plague. We're the first group of young adults to see our friends sicken and die from it.

VERONICA CHAMBERS

We came of age with the terrifying knowledge that unsafe sex could kill us. "

"If you are in **emotional** pain, it is important that you be able to **forgive.** ...Consider the alternative. If you are unable to forgive, you create a **blockage** in your life—a low-grade anger that **permeates** your whole view of the world. Perhaps you can live with this blockage—half the world does —but your life will never be completely pleasant because the **hurt and anger** you feel will keep coming up. And its **impact** will not just be limited to the person who hurt you; it will **spread to everyone** who vaguely resembles the offender. "

ZOLEKA ADAMS

Model used for illustration only

"When I'm not weeping over this color madness, I silently scream, 'When will it end?'"

...Right now, the last plantation is the mind. We need an ongoing dialogue in every Black home to discuss the issue of colorism among us, conflict with other ethnic groups of color—remember, we are going to be the majority one day..."

ITABARI NJERI

73

"Some of us have been brainwashed into thinking that some women '*just like to be hit.*'

I can testify that **I have never heard any sister express the opinion that she liked to be hit,** that she saw hitting as a gesture of love.

Our leaders do not focus on the issue of Black male violence against women. **We can take a stand against domestic violence only by first acknowledging that it exists—that it is a** problem in Black life.

Black women must work harder than any other group in the society to value our bodies, our selves and our lives. **When we challenge Black male violence we are expressing our love of ourselves and our people.** This love heals and liberates us all."

bell hooks

why some people be mad at me sometimes

they ask me to remember

but they want me to remember

their memories and I keep on

remembering mine.

LUCILLE CLIFTON

"During a particularly trying time, I asked my extended family to come together. We joined hands in a circle, **asking God for guidance and patience** through what we knew would be a long struggle. And when I looked up, I glanced at a shelf and saw that old photograph of me and [my sister]. I recalled a theory I once heard **that mentally ill people are really old souls from heaven,** the bravest ones, who volunteer to be born on earth with defects so they can teach important lessons to those of us who are more fortunate. I knew then that **my sister had been here with the purpose.** It was so that I could better understand the person for whom we prayed that day and fight to save a life."

BRENDA LANE RICHARDSON

"...We are not made of stone.

There is a space in our hearts carved out for all the

are gone too soon from our lives, but

whose deep notes still flow

In the memory of them *we keep holding on."*

We break, falter, feel lonely.

fathers, uncles, cousins, sons and lovers who

rough us, whose songs we will remember every day.

NATASHA TARPLEY

"Everybody ought to take a day off, not just from the job, but from family, friends, from everything, and sit down and think. Now that takes courage....

The world is not going to end or fall apart....If you can't get everybody out of the house, go sit in a church, or the park, or take a long walk...Call it a healing day."

MAYA ANGELOU

HAVING WHAT MATTERS

I n our annual wealth-building issue, I wrote about the need for us as a people to be frugal and to plan for long-term financial stability—remember my 1989 van with the coat-hanger antenna? In the past I've also stressed the importance of "me time"—time to nourish and reconnect with self, something we sisters aren't quick to do. Well, those two themes met head-on in my life recently as I was finishing my new book, *Having What Matters: The Black Woman's Guide to Creating the Life You Really Want.* I knew I could go on being the editor of the nation's number one magazine for Black women, running my three businesses, remaining active in my community, and being a "present" wife and mother. But I also knew that I, Monique, would always be at the end of my very long to-do list, especially since my husband and I were about to launch our fourth business venture, Akwaaba by the Sea, the only Black-owned inn in the historic seaside resort of Cape May, New Jersey.

In a moment of reflection, I realized I no longer wanted to live life in a rush, shortchanging myself to meet all my other obligations. The time had clearly come to embrace change: I made the hard decision to leave ESSENCE.

When I told my 9-year-old daughter, Glynn, that Mommy would no longer be at ESSENCE, she looked alarmed and shouted, "Why?" I was stunned by her reaction and reminded her that she'd always wanted me to pick her up from school and help her with homework. Now I would be able to, I told her. "But how are we going to live in this house and have food on the table?" she asked with concern.

Her questions made sense: Every time I couldn't accompany her class on a trip, or had to work late for the fourth night in a week, or go away on business, I would explain that Mommy had to work so we could afford the things we needed. Now I delighted in explaining to her that our frugal, bootstrapping ways—her going without the latest brand-name sneakers; Mommy's and Daddy's working full-time jobs while struggling to build our own small businesses—had made it possible for me to come home and oversee our company with full confidence that our financial needs would be met.

With her fears put to rest, she asked excitedly, "Does this mean we'll all sit down and have dinner together as a family?" When I said yes, she squeezed my neck in such a way that

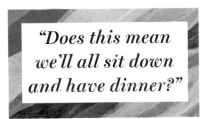

"Does this mean we'll all sit down and have dinner?"

there was no mistaking how much that mattered to her. I hugged her back, because it matters just as much to me.

My time here has been more than a job for me. It has been an extraordinary mission—a chance to make Black people's lives better through the pages of ESSENCE. In the future, I'll continue this mission by providing a place for my sisters and brothers to relax and revive their spirits—something I'm looking forward to doing more of myself.

Monique Greenwood

Monique Greenwood
Editor-in-Chief
October 2001

"I learned a long time ago that when you've had some success, it's not enough to just sit back and enjoy it. You've got to reach back and pull someone else up too. I keep that lesson with me every day, whether it's as the first lady, as a woman or as a mom. I tell my girls all the time that they are beautiful, that they are smart and that they should live life without fear of failing. I say these things because they are absolutely true..."

"The earlier you realize
you can build a career
that affects the community,
the easier it becomes
to shape it."

MICHELLE OBAMA

"Do the one thing you think you cannot do.

FAIL AT IT. TRY AGAIN.

Do better the second time.

The only people who never tumble are those who never mount the high wire."

OPRAH WINFREY

"YOU WILL
NEVER REGRET:
SAYING NO WHEN
YOU REALLY
WANT TO SAY NO.

A MANTRA I LIVE BY:

Be relentless.
Be excellent.
And own your ambition."

ROXANE GAY

Sheila C. Johnson at her Virginia Salamander Resort & Spa

SHEILA'S 10 GOLDEN RULES

1 If you don't know who you are, don't attempt to start a business.

2 God is in the details: Make a plan, sign every check and know your employees.

3 Be careful whom you bring into your environment. They cannot come in with their own agenda.

4 The same skills it takes to manage the books of a household can be applied to running a business.

5 Don't be afraid of the big investment.

6 Whether you have two cents or a fortune, keep your eye on the ball, because people will rob you blind.

7 Beware of energy vampires.

8 Know when it's time to let go, whether it's a business or a relationship.

9 Do not open your kimono about your personal life, because people will take advantage of your weaknesses.

10 Lead with integrity.

SHEILA C. JOHNSON

"Dream big.
Work hard.

ALL
THINGS
ARE
POSSIBLE."

URSULA M. BURNS

Vanessa Williams at home

"Whatever you do, you
    have to remain focused and
    committed to whatever it is
    you want to accomplish.
    Always be prepared.
    Always be your best.
    Always be professional.
    Never stop learning.
    It will pay off."

VANESSA WILLIAMS

"It takes personal security to be able to

stand in that place of conflict,

where people differ, and still be able to

listen respectfully,

question yourself and still

come out whole."

KATHERINE TYLER SCOTT

"No matter where
and how we work,
**we're always in business
for ourselves."**

JOSEFINA SANDS

"All great outward **triumphs** begin from **within** as we locate **the core** of who we are and play it for all it's **worth.** And that, my dear sister, makes every **struggle** you ever experience **PRICELESS!"**

MICHELLE McKINNEY HAMMOND

"The key to happiness is not being concerned with what other people **think** about you.

If I believe the good things, then I have to believe the bad. So I have to **stop believing** any of it."

SHONDA RHIMES

"The best answers I've discovered are the ones that sisters who came long before me—and who didn't have squat to their names but were wealthy in wisdom—always knew: Show the ones you love that you love them. Get out of your hurry. Decide what matters to you and then boldly rearrange your life to have at it. Know that you're already worth something. Want what you already have....Consider what it would feel like to stop buying and start being."

MICHELLE BURFORD

109

"I just think
there's nothing
we can't do.
I've never
considered it to be a
disadvantage to be a
Black woman.
I've never
wanted to be
anything else.
We have brains!
We're beautiful!
We should be able to
do anything
we set our minds to!"

DIANA ROSS

PURPOSE

GETTING DOWN

I f anyone had told me then that life is a journey not a destination, I don't know if I could have been able to have heard, much less understood. But, oh my sisters, I am here to tell you that I can now bear witness to the wisdom of those words. At last my stuttering spirit can speak freely. And for that I have to thank you and ESSENCE. How can I begin to tell you all the things I've learned, the spiritual, intellectual and emotional growth and changes I've been through as a result of having had the privilege to serve as the editor-in-chief for nine of these ten years? Had the opportunity to develop and work on a magazine about Black women—"For Today's Black Woman." A magazine about me. It gave me the confidence to be myself. Got the chance to explore myriad dimensions of our collective and my individual being. Never been a boss before I became one here. Made me grow up, grow proud and it's humbled me. Have met people whose names I once read with awe and learned firsthand that people are people—if we just be real. Have ego tripped and tripped over my ego. Have walked with the powerful and have had my share of power. Found it scary, spoiling, have handled it poor and well. And as a result have learned the meaning of responsibility though I have not always been the responsible being I'd like to be.

All of which has brought me to the point that I now am wholly committed to seeing my life as a journey and not as a destination. I now understand why the old folks in the church I grew up in would sing with so many mixed emotions that song about Jacob's ladder. "We are climbing Jacob's ladder—every rung goes higher,

higher!" Have come to understand that I am but a pilgrim. Learned to talk to God and to be open to hear the spirit whisper in my soul. Have reopened my eyes like a child's—wide and full of hope and wonder. Have learned to honor the spirits of my ancestors and to believe in the presence of "things unseen." Come to understand that everyone we meet is a teacher and have felt blessed because I have sat at the feet of people I consider to be among the prophets of our times.

My wish for you is what I wish for me—that wherever our life's journeys take us we walk good and be true to ourselves and our people. That we be preservers of life. That we dream and work to make our dream a reality. That we value people more than things. That we African-Americans be proud of who we are—and what we came from. That we strengthen our spirits and our resolve to overcome oppression in all its ugly forms. That we keep our eyes set on the North Star no matter where we journey, 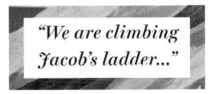 so that freedom stays on our minds. That no matter how high we climb up Jacob's ladder or how low we may think we fall, we remember that we are one people, one heart, one spirit, one love!

Again, life is a journey not a destination—so walk good my sisters. Let your sweet spirits shine!

Marcia Ann Gillespie

Marcia Ann Gillespie
Editor-in-Chief
May 1980

HERITAGE

My mother

never taught me

to build

sand castles.

She taught me

to build pyramids

erected from the sand

as monuments to...

our people

our past.

LISA BOND BREWER

117

"SIMPLY PUT,
WE HAVE
TO FEEL GOOD
TO DO GOOD.

...Do it now. Every day you delay puts you that much farther from reaching your goal, from achieving your vision. Work at your dreams and watch how your newfound energy empowers you to do anything, be anything, get anything you want."

VICTORIA JOHNSON

"(He) told me that I needed more education because the public school I'd gone to hadn't done a good job of preparing me for a job...He told me to read a newspaper every day, and he recommended other books. I had to have a dictionary next to me as I read.
...Sometimes I rewrote things ten times, but he told me, 'I know that you're going to make it; you just need help. You have what I look for in every employee: **determination, discipline and dedication.**'"

JILL BULLOCK

"...When I had to decide about the word

feminist for myself, it just didn't fit,

especially when you had to say

Black feminist.

... I wanted a word that was ***visible*** in itself,

because it came out of my ***own*** culture

womanist

...I thought about how **Black women** always say to their daughters, 'you're acting womanish,' which is the *foundation* of our *self-love* as Black women. ....You could be a ***womanist***, period. **You are the center of your world."**

womanist

ALICE WALKER

"I read the Bible.
It didn't say just go to church.
It said,
'Do something.'"

CHARLESZETTA "MOTHER" WADDLES

Community volunteers

"I tell them that there are
three kinds
of people in the world:
those who make things happen,
those who watch things happen and
those who wonder what happened."

ANNA SINGLETON

"**We really have to begin to form movements again.** America does something that's real tricky to people, and that's if it can, it will turn everybody into tribes—you know, factions. And so it always comes down to a Black-white issue. But when you talk to Mexican-Americans they talk about police brutality. When you talk to Puerto Ricans they talk about police brutality. **This time what we have to do is really make a movement involving peoples of color that really** does address the big issues of race as they affect all kinds of brown and beige and yellow people in this country..."

MARCIA ANN GILLESPIE

"YOU CAN'T GET SHAKEN IN THE WORST POSSIBLE MOMENT.

YOU HAVE TO HAVE THE VISION TO SEE BEYOND THE SHORT TERM."

MELLODY HOBSON

"So where do we go from here? I'm asking you what I'm asking myself: What's up with us? Just who are we, and what is our purpose? What are we living for? Willing to die for?

And who will sustain us, individually and as a people, if not our children? It's the midnight hour, but it's not too late to turn on the light."

SUSAN L. TAYLOR

"I realized that
I owed my children.
I owed them peace of mind
and a better life.
I was determined that
they should have it."

SONIA P. BROOKS-OMULEPU

135

"...We're essentially conditioned not to resist authority.

We are conditioned to go along to get along. We're conditioned to believe that if we're quiet now, we will ultimately be in a better position to do justice—to do the right thing later. The problem with this, though, is that if you're socialized to be quiet now, what makes you think that you will ever be socialized to speak out later?"

LANI GUINIER

"We complain among ourselves about how Black victims of crime are treated as less important... but we seldom let anyone else know it. We berate the portrayal of Black people on television shows, but we watch them anyway....

Our critical silence is not enough.

We have to become actively involved in responding to how the media covers us.

...It's time for us to stop being accomplices in our own victimization."

JERI L. LOVE

"What is at
the summit of
courage, I think
it is freedom. The
freedom that comes
with the knowledge that
no earthly power can break
you; that an unbroken spirit is
the only thing that you cannot
live without; that in the end it is
the courage of conviction that moves
things; that makes all change possible."

PAULA GIDDINGS

"*Sometimes the only reward for trying to do right is a clear conscience.*"

OCTAVIA E. BUTLER

LEGACY

HEAVEN ON EARTH

I learned so much during the time of my mother's transition. Seeing my beloved Babs slip away devastated me, but it was also a time of deep revelation. It was then I first grasped that our own lives require a vast measure of our love and devotion. I spent countless hours at my mother's bedside, listening to her, caring for her, learning from the wise elders who surrounded her. What I discovered sliced like a laser through the tangle of my delusions: Heaven is here on earth; it's now. We cheat ourselves when we disregard this.

Older people know this best. They see more clearly that their sorrows and suffering mostly came from worrying, and in retrospect, they understand that every worry was unnecessary because God was always working things out. I've heard so many older folks echo this same regret—that they neglected to make time for themselves, never pausing to listen to their own longings. Their years were filled with work, worry and doing for others, and not until age and arthritis slowed them did they become more reflective and concerned with what would bring them fulfillment and inner peace. They wished then that they had been more courageous, aiming higher for themselves and not only for their loved ones. As my own Babs hovered on the margin of her life, I saw how much she, too, had sacrificed for us, yet she died without ever singing her own song.

This very evening, kick off your shoes, put your feet up, and reconnect with your soul. It is the larger Self, the source of the wisdom within you. Our soul never forgets what it came here to do. Ask yourself, How would I feel if I courageously let go of all anger and disappointment about the past and my fear and anxiety about the future? How would I seek, serve and love this year if I believed I was perfectly and permanently secure in the arms of God? Sit with these questions for a few evenings and listen to your soul with an open heart. We stay stuck and fearful when we forget our own divinity, but as we come home to God in us, we begin to trust the gentle kindness and balance of the universe, the hardness in us softens, our fears dissolve...

Be the Light that was born as you. Begin by naming your dreams, what you do best, what gives you the most fulfillment. Visualize yourself living your dreams, lofty ones. Black people must have big dreams to effect big changes. Keep that vision strong by revisiting it often. Make a list of the actions required to achieve your goals, and step boldly onto the path. Our desires are the will of God for us. Wherever they take us, the grace of God will protect and fulfill us...

"Listen to your soul."

This is the year to discipline your mind, strengthen your will and become a vessel God can use. As we grasp that heaven is right here on earth, we will create an individual and collective revolution! We can shape a life of our choosing, even as we help uplift our community, help heal our world. At the end of the day, our lives will be a mirror of our dreams and desires—not the ones we shrank from and fearfully denied, but the ones we answered, to which we brought our energy and passion, and into which we breathed life, calmly trusting the perfection of God's plan.

Susan L. Taylor

Susan L. Taylor
Editor-in-Chief Emerita
Editorial Director
January 2008

"Black women are nurturers.
We nurture our families by
seriously listening to and seriously
considering what they tell us."

SAMELLA LEWIS

149

"Remember your roots, your history and the forbearers shoulders on which you stand. And pass them on to your children and to other Black children whose parents may not be able to. As a Black community today we have no greater priority than ensuring the rootedness of all of our children—poor, middle-class and Ivy League.

Young people who do not know where they come from and the struggle it took to get them where they are now will not know where they are going or what to do for anyone besides themselves if and when they finally arrive somewhere.

Tubman, a Sojourner Truth, a Frederick Douglass from slavery, a Benjamin Mays and Martin Luther King Jr. and Fannie Lou Hamer from segregation—people who helped transform America from a theoretical into a more living democracy."

MARIAN WRIGHT EDELMAN

"We must encourage and reinvigorate dedication
among African-American teachers who would
be willing, in spite of the obstacles, to educate
the next generation.

I've been a teacher for more than 25 years, and
my students often ask, 'Why are you a teacher?'
implying that I've made a terrible career choice.
I tell them, 'I teach because once upon a time a teacher
made a difference in my life, so I'm here to make a
difference for you.'

Our children deserve the best, brightest, most capable
teachers. They also deserve highly accomplished African-
American teachers who understand where they are
coming from as well as where we need to be.

…A Black child sits in a classroom today—hopeful,
enthusiastic, curious. In that child sleeps the vision and
wisdom of our people. Only the touch of a dedicated and
well-trained teacher can awaken it."

SHARON M. DRAPER

"Teach our children the importance

of getting a good education.

While not a guarantee of success,

education is a precondition to survival

in America today."

MARIAN WRIGHT EDELMAN

"PUT SUCCESS AND FAILURE IN THEIR PROPER CONTEXTS.

Encourage your child to strive for the best in life, but don't burden her too early with your value judgments about what constitutes a successful individual. Allow her to make her own decisions about the tasks or activities she wants to pursue. Above all, take care that the values you teach your child go beyond the materialistic definition of success; make sure that she knows there is more to life than making money.

LOOK TO OUR HERITAGE AND TRADITIONS FOR VALUES.

Stress such qualities as spirituality, cooperation, personal dignity and the love and protection of family as values to which we should all aspire."

MONIQUE BURNS

"It is our job to fulfill the primary goal of parenting, which is to bring our children to independence. It is our job to love our children so much that we will give them more of what we know they need than of what they think they want."

ELAINE BROWN

Models used for illustration only

Models used for illustration only

"There's only one thing that I am, at this moment in my life, completely certain of: I will do all in my power to make sure that my daughter will not learn what I learned; that she will not be looked upon by eyes that see her only in pieces, eyes that dismantle

and redact and finally discard her. I will not have that happen to her as it happened to me, unprepared and unarmed. Because I'm going to tell her all the things I experienced, all the things I didn't."

asha bandele

"THE WHOLE WORLD WON'T BE MINE THIS TIME.

There are books and plays I am not going to write because I am raising a wondrous daughter, alone. There are horses I am not going to ride, fascinating friends I am not going to have; brown eyes that won't be peering into mine. I am beginning to get it.

I AM LEARNING TO SAY YES TO THE CHOICES I HAVE MADE.

Find my dreams there, where I am extremely myself. I look like I am walking fast, but I just hit my stride; a gait I can handle."

Ntozake Shange

*"**Everything** that happens, every person who shows up and every **situation** in our lives occurs because on some level **we called it** to ourselves. When we **understand** this, we can begin to **move beyond** just*

holding ourselves together in the face of life's *difficulties*. We can begin to see our very *challenges as opportunities* to demonstrate, to create, to be *who we really are*—a giant, beautiful reflection of *love*."

TARA ROBERTS

"I've realized that all I have in the world is MY

INTEGRITY, and

when I say one

thing and do another I do injury to an

essential part of MYSELF."

JILL NELSON

"...You make
all these great
calculations
about your life

—where you
want to be in
so many years,

how you want
to get there
and what to
take with you.

But sooner or
later it hits you
that in this life
there are no
guarantees.

Everything is a risk.

In the end, all you can really count
on is what comes through
faith and prayer."

CAROLYN

"Forget about trying to get through the storms.

Life is about learning

to dance in the rain."

TAMIA

171

"I pray for a SOUND mind, UNBROKEN WORK fit for my soul, GOOD JUSTICE for my peopl

RENITA J. WEEMS

health,

LOVING,

and for every sister contemplating
death, a reason for

LIVING—
WHOLE."

Susan L. Taylor

CONTRIBUTORS

*Essence reader identified by first
 name only

Paula Giddings

Marcia Ann Gillespie

Nikki Giovanni

Hattie Gossett

Monique Greenwood

Lani Guinier

Mellody Hobson

bell hooks

Dr. Gwendolyn Goldsby Grant

Michelle McKinney Hammond

Victoria Johnson

Sheila C. Johnson

Ziba Kashef

Rae Lewis-Thornton

Samella Lewis

Audre Lorde

Jeri L. Love

Louise Meriwether

Jill Nelson

Itabari Njeri

Michelle Obama

*Debbie P.

Retha Powers

Shonda Rhimes

Brenda Lane Richardson

Robin Roberts

Tara Roberts

Regina R. Robertson

Diana Ross

*Donnie S.

Josefina Sands

Jill Scott

Katherine Tyler Scott

Ntozake Shange

Anna Singleton

Natasha Tarpley

Tamia

Susan L. Taylor

Iyanla Vanzant

Charleszetta "Mother" Waddles

Dr. Brenda Wade

Alice Walker

Renita J. Weems

Vanessa Williams

Oprah Winfrey

Your Faith Walk
Credits

2 Chester Higgins; **11** *Gifted*, Natasha Wescoat; **15** Lauri Lyons; **16** Photolyric/Getty Images; **18** Trinette Reed/Offset; **20** *Shango*, Bisa Butler; **22** Jefry Andres Wright; **25** Cavan Images/ Offset; **28** Inti St. Clair/Getty Images; **31** *The Phoenix II*, Bisa Butler; **35** Myles Kwesi Hutchful; **37** nambitomo/iStockphoto/Getty Images; **39** Lauren Crew; **40-41** BZB/Getty Images; **43** Buena Vista Images/The Image Bank/Getty Images; **45** Vito Palmisano/Getty Images; **46** Jon Naso/NY Daily News Archive via Getty Images; **49** Sam Edwards/Getty Images; **52-53** Background photo: Tetra Images/Getty Images, Inset photo: Courtesy of Lucille Clifton Estate; **55** Jirard; **59** Comstock Images via Getty Images; **61** Kwesi Abbensetts **62-63** Kathy Collins/Getty Images; **64-65** Jen Everett; **66** David W. Johnson; **67** Inset: ESSENCE Magazine, December 1994 cover; **70-71** Zave Smith/Image Source/ Corbis; **73** Clockwise: Hosea Johnson, Rolf Bruderer/Blend Images/Corbis, Michael Rowe; **74** Ron Zmiri/Shutterstock; **77** Simon Frederick; **78** *Faith*, Henry Lee Battle, henryleebattle.com; **82-83** Granger Wootz/Blend Images/ Getty Images; **85** *June Tree*, Natasha Wescoat; **88** Marc Baptiste/Corbis Outline; **94** Eli M Kaplan; **98** Kwaku Alston/Corbis Outline; **103** Blend Images/Alamy **105** Photo ephemera/Getty Images; **109** Luis Alvarez/Getty Images **110** JenniferPhotographyimaging Getty Images; **113** *Blue Willow*, Natasha Wescoat; **117** *Not Just Fitting End*, Nathaniel Donnett; **121** AmmentorpDK/iStockphoto/ Getty Images; **125** Hill Street Studios/Eric Raptosh/Blend Images/Corbis; **126** Jen Everett; **128-129** Tayarisha Poe; **132-133** Ed Morris/Getty Images; **135** Kelvin Murray/Getty Images; **136** Nabil K. Mark/Centre Daily Times/TNS via Getty Images; **140-141** Klaus Vedfelt/Getty Images **142-143** Tayarisha Poe; **1** *Night and Day II*, Natasha Wesco **148-149** Michelle Braxton; **151** *Lo the Way You Love Yourself Luv: A.J.*, Nathaniel Donnett; **152** Fror top: Stock Connection/Supersto .com, Cavan Images/Offset; **154** Comstock/Getty Images; **156** *A Mother's Love*, Evita Tezeno, evitatezeno.com; **159** Adreinne Waheed; **160-161** Jerry Taliaferro; **163** *AfroDite*, Bis Butler; **167** Zayna Daze; **170-171** Jonathan Knowles/Getty Images **174** Lauri Lyons